THIS IS BASEBALL

by Margaret Blackstone
pictures by John O'Brien

Henry Holt and Company ◆ New York

For my father, Henry
my son, Dash
my husband, Tom
and my brothers, Pete and Neil
all great boys of summer
and for my friend, Elissa
one of the great girls of all seasons
—M.B.

For Tessie,
the first in my lineup
—J.O'B.

Published by Henry Holt and Company, Inc., 115 West 18th Street, New York, New York 10011.
Published simultaneously in Canada by Fitzhenry & Whiteside Ltd., 195 Allstate Parkway, Markham, Ontario L3R 4T8.

Library of Congress Cataloging-in-Publication Data
Blackstone, Margaret / This is baseball / by Margaret Blackstone; pictures by John O'Brien.
Summary: A simple introduction to the game of baseball, covering its equipment, players,
and basic plays. The illustrations show a game in progress. ISBN 0-8050-2390-9
1. Baseball—Juvenile literature. [1. Baseball.] I. O'Brien, John, ill. II. Title. GV867.5.B57 1993 796.357—dc20 92-22921

Printed in the United States of America on acid-free paper. ∞

3 5 7 9 10 8 6 4

THIS IS BASEBALL

This is a stadium,

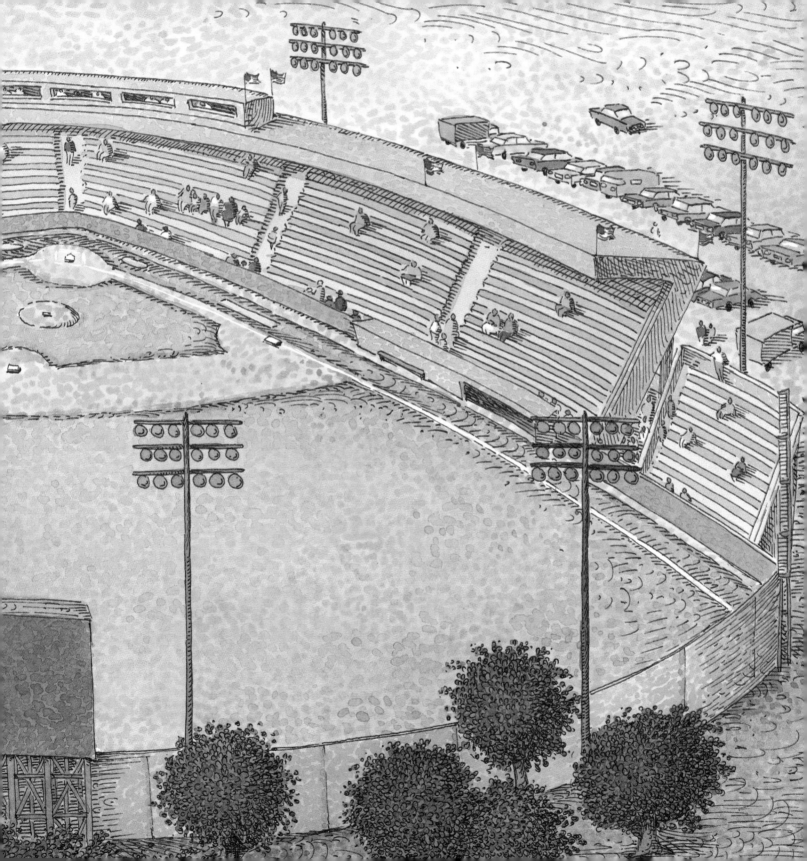

and this is a baseball diamond.

This is one team,

and this is the other.

These are the fans.

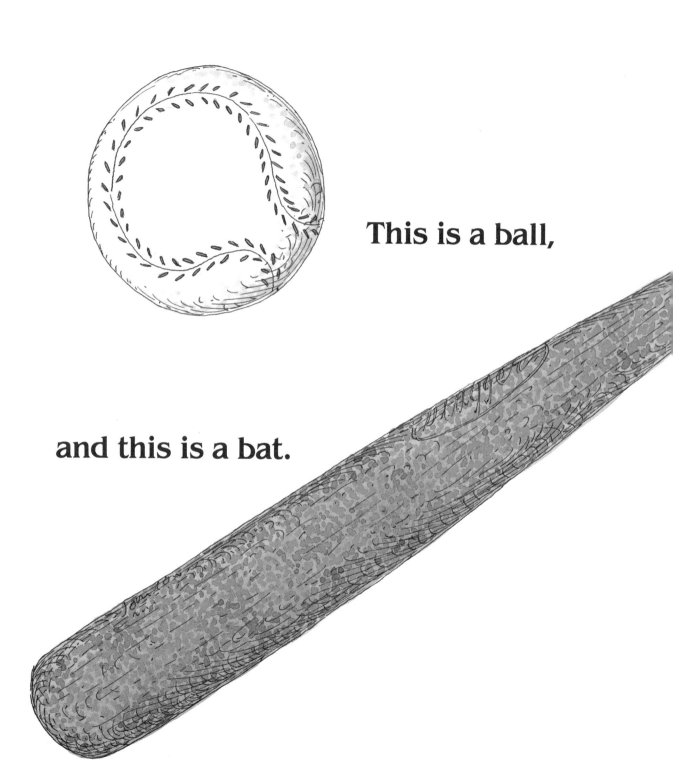

This is a ball,

and this is a bat.

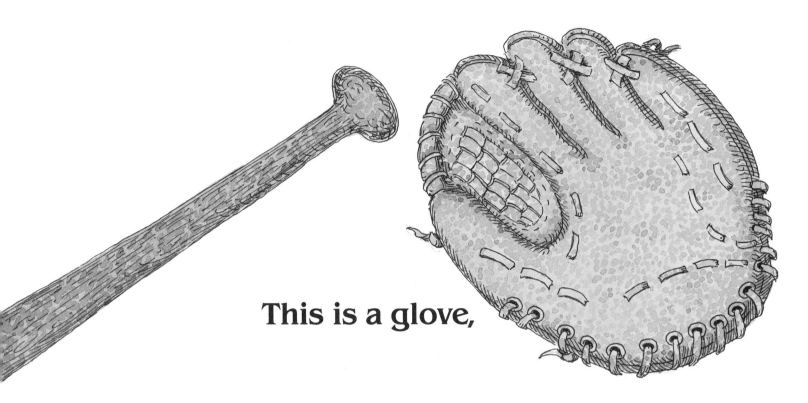

This is a glove,

and this is a cap.

This is a player.

And these are the umpires who call the game.

This is a pitcher.

This is a catcher.

This is the infield.

This is the outfield.

This is a pitch.

And this is a hit!

This is a high fly ball to deep left field...

and this is a
HOME RUN!

This team has won,

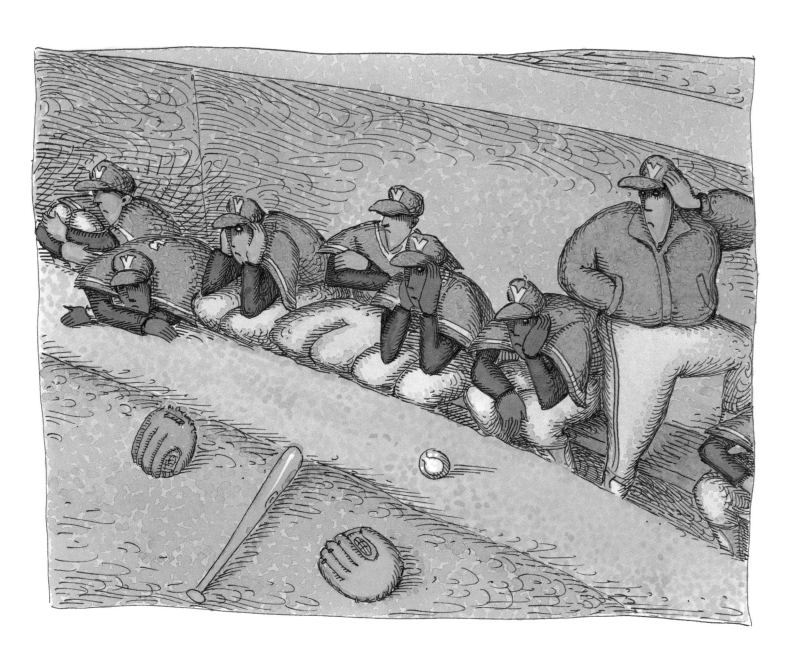

and this team has lost.

Tomorrow there will be another game.